kWh

Electricity Saving 'Gadgets'

This can help save electricity.

SUPER EFFICIENCY RATING

The more stars the more energy efficient

ENERGY RATING ®

A joint government and industry program

Energy consumption

670

kWh per year

Based on 10 hrs daily use in recommended home viewing picture mode and tested in accordance with AS/NZS 62087.2.2

TVs displayed for sale may be set in a display mode that may consume more energy than the rating above indicates and may be brighter. Energy consumption and running costs will depend on how you adjust and use this TV.

Compare models at www.energyrating.gov.au

3

This car can save electricity.

This computer can save electricity.

This light can save electricity.

This globe can save electricity.

This stop sign can save electricity.

STOP

4-WAY

13

This stop light can save electricity.

15

This can save electricity too.